MG 1945-1964
PHOTO ARCHIVE

MG 1945-1964
PHOTO ARCHIVE

David A. Knowles

Iconografix
Photo Archive Series

Iconografix
PO Box 609
Osceola, Wisconsin 54020 USA

Text Copyright © 1996

Library of Congress Card Number 96-76222

ISBN 1-882256-52-2

96 97 98 99 00 5 4 3 2 1

Cover and book design by Lou Gordon, Osceola, Wisconsin

Printed in the United States of America

Book trade distribution by Voyageur Press, Inc. (800) 888-9653

PREFACE

The histories of machines and mechanical gadgets are contained in the books, journals, correspondence, and personal papers stored in libraries and archives throughout the world. Written in tens of languages, covering thousands of subjects, the stories are recorded in millions of words.

Words are powerful. Yet, the impact of a single image, a photograph or an illustration, often relates more than dozens of pages of text. Fortunately, many of the libraries and archives that house the words also preserve the images.

In the *Photo Archive Series*, Iconografix reproduces photographs and illustrations selected from public and private collections. The images are chosen to tell a story—to capture the character of their subject. Reproduced as found, they are accompanied by the captions made available by the archive.

The Iconografix *Photo Archive Series* is dedicated to young and old alike, the enthusiast, the collector and anyone, who like us, is fascinated by "things" mechanical.

ACKNOWLEDGMENTS

We wish to acknowledge the contributions of Cliff Bray, Jimmy Cox, Graham Robson, Bob West, and Dickie Wright.

The classic lines of the TC Midget have earned it a place in sports car folklore, including the epithet *The Sports Car America Loved First.*

INTRODUCTION

Page 9 left hand column

The M.G. marque began to take shape in the university town of Oxford, England, in the early 1920s. The true M.G. ancestors were a series of specially modified Morris cars, produced at William Morris's own Morris Garages business. The Morris Garages, managed on Morris' behalf by Cecil Kimber, gave rise to the M.G. name which was applied to these specials from 1923.

Predecessor of the TC was this TA, launched in 1936.

The 1920s and 1930s saw the business expand. By 1929, it was necessary to move to new premises at the nearby town of Abingdon-upon-Thames, in order to build a new model, the M-Type Midget. Soon afterwards, on July 21, 1930, the M.G. Car Company Ltd. was registered as a company in its own right. By this time, the cars which carried the M.G. name were no longer warmed over Morris Oxfords. Although they still owed their allegiance to Morris Motors, some of them had become thoroughbreds in their own right.

Racing successes in the early 1930s brought considerable fame and glory to the M.G. name. On July 1, 1935 Morris, by then ennobled as Lord Nuffield, transferred various private business interests—including M.G.—to the ownership and management of Morris Motors. At a stroke, M.G. lost its independence and the exciting but very expensive racing programme was curtailed. Development began of a less exotic, but far more commercially sensible range of M.G. cars. Foremost amongst these new cars was the T-Series Midget, announced in the spring of 1936. The first T-Series, later to be known as the TA, was controversial in the eyes of some die-hard M.G. enthusiasts, not only because it was designed at Cowley rather than at Abingdon but also because it used more mundane components from the Morris Motors parts bin. However, the recipe was clearly a successful one. M.G. output more than doubled from a low in 1935 to almost 3,000 cars in 1937, of which exports accounted for just 430 sales. This sort of output—very respectable but hardly earth-shattering—might have continued at similar levels, had not the political troubles brewing in Europe erupted into war in September 1939. With Britain at war with Germany, domestic car production fizzled out in 1940 and the factories were turned over to more pressing production needs.

POST-WAR: EXPORT TO SURVIVE

As the war in Europe drew to a close in 1945, M.G. was able to turn its attention to car production again. However, Cecil Kimber, M.G.'s guiding light from the start, had been dismissed in 1941 following a management fallout. He died tragically in a railway accident four years later, so M.G.'s post-war future lay in different hands. Responsibility at Cowley for M.G. affairs was given to H. A. Ryder, a Morris Motors director since 1926. Ryder came from Morris Radiators branch and knew very little of car production. When asked what M.G. should build, he suggested, logically enough, that it would be simplest to start where the factory had left off, with the TB Midget, just 379 examples of which had been built before war had stopped production. Someone sensibly suggested that it would be wise to correct what problems there had been in service with the TA and TB. As these had been mostly complaints about the interior width and problems with the front suspension, it was these features which were altered in the develop-ment of the TC Midget.

The post-war British economy was in tatters, the result of bleeding the coffers dry for the war effort. Britain's car manufacturers were forced—both through lack of local customers (rationing and taxes) and government edict (materials for export production)—to ship a larger proportion of their output overseas. M.G. was unquestionably aided in this endeavour by the fact that US servicemen, posted in Britain and occupied Germany, had discovered the joys of the simple, elegant, and sprightly M.G. sports car. Year on year, post-war M.G. production climbed rapidly, and export sales—in particular sales to US service personnel and eventually direct to the USA itself—took off dramatically. In later years, it would be fond memories of the M.G. TC which gave rise to the famous advertising slogan *M.G.—The Sports Car America Loved First*.

In the wake of the distinctly pre-war design of the TC came the mechanically more modern YA saloon, with independent front suspension. In January 1950, the men at Abingdon took a YA chassis, cut five inches out of it and formed the basis of the new TD Midget. From this point, with production for the USA dominating output, M.G. never looked back. From 1950, when over 7,000 M.G. cars were built, output grew to 11,000 per annum within five years.

North American sports car enthusiasts had taken to the little M.G. sports car in a big way, largely inspired by the writings of people like John Bond of *Road and Track*, and the successes of drivers with TCs and TDs at places such as Lime Rock and Sebring. Flushed with their success, the people at Abingdon argued the case for being given back some of the autonomy which they had so jealously guarded prior to July 1935. At first, their arguments fell on deaf ears. Despite their protestations, their own ideas for a brand new aerodynamic successor to the TD were turned down, forcing them to hastily concoct the TF Midget. The TF was given a lukewarm reception by the public and press alike, which is rather ironic when one considers that nowadays this model is regarded by many as one of the most beautiful M.G. sports cars built.

WIND OF CHANGE AT ABINGDON:
THE AERODYNAMIC MGA

Falling sales of the TF, coupled with pressure from several quarters and, to an extent, changes of attitude in the wake of the Austin/Morris merger of 1952, rapidly led to common sense prevailing. M.G. gained a greater degree of control over its own destiny in June 1954, when a drawing office was established at Abingdon. Within a year, M.G. was back at Le Mans, racing three prototypes of Syd Enever's sleekly styled MGA sports car.

The launch of the MGA in September 1955 heralded another period of dramatic growth at Abingdon. Whilst it was an MGA which marked the production of the 100,000th car at Abingdon in March 1956, it would only be six years before the 100,000th example of the MGA itself would roll off the production lines. In the intervening period, the men at M.G. rekindled their pre-war record-breaking habits, and there were memorable visits in 1957 and 1959 to the salt-flats of Utah near Wendover.

With export success in mind, M.G. was able to turn its attention to a successor for the MGA. It emerged in September 1962 as the monocoque-bodied MGB, alongside the technically interesting M.G. 1100 saloon, with its novel Hydrolastic fluid suspension system. In the meantime, the "adopted" Austin-Healey Sprite of 1958 spawned the M.G. Midget of 1961. Although M.G. production had dipped from the 1957 peak to a low of 14,000 in 1960—a consequence not only of the switch of Austin-Healey production to Abingdon in 1957 but also of a sales recession in the USA—the MGB saw production soar again to over 37,000 by 1964, the final year covered by this volume. By this time, M.G.—and its parent the British Motor Corporation—was on a roll, and it seemed as if nothing could stop it.

An M.G. TC chassis goes down the production line at Abingdon.

This is a pre-war photograph of the prototype for the M.G. YA, known at this stage as the M.G. Ten.

The styling of the M.G. Y-Type was clearly rooted in pre-war thinking, as this 1940 photograph proves.

A trailer load of four Y-Type bodies.

The Y-Type was entered in a number of events; this was the 1954 Monte Carlo entry of Gregor Grant and George Phillips.

Launched in October 1948, the YT Tourer was an attempt to cash in on the demand for an open four-seater M.G., in the vein of the pre-war VA Tourer. In production for less than two years, only 877 of this relatively unsuccessful car were built.

Here the new YT Tourer poses amongst a number of Nuffield products, including a Cowley-designed prototype for an M.G. Midget based upon the Morris Minor.

Continental European coachbuilders tried their hand at rebodying the Y-Type. This Zagato offering was—well—interesting.

The rear view of the Zagato Y-Type shows that, whilst undoubtedly modern for its day, it was not that practical—there was no boot lid, for example!

Whereas the TC Midget had been largely based upon the TB, the last pre-war Midget, the TD Midget was developed using the chassis of the Y-Series saloon. This is an early car, possibly a pre-production car of 1949, identifiable by the slotted wheel hubs.

Although instantly recognisable as an M.G., the TD was less classically proportioned than the TC. It was, however, unquestionably a dynamically superior car.

M.G. TD Midgets proceed along the manual production line. Abingdon never became mechanised in this respect.

EX172, a special bodied M.G. TD Midget built at Abingdon for the 1951 Le Mans race.

The team of M.G. staff pose alongside EX172 in the summer of 1951. George Phillips, for whom the car was built, is at the wheel, whilst M.G.'s Chief Engineer Syd Enever stands alongside him.

George Phillips driving EX172. Note how strange the driver looked perched high above the low and sleek body—
a legacy of the TD chassis.

Whilst Gerald Palmer experimented with ideas for a monocoque M.G. sports car at Cowley, Syd Enever and his team at Abingdon, with help from Eric Carter of Morris Motors' Bodies Branch, created this car, EX175, using a new chassis and running gear adapted from the TD Midget.

Here EX175 is seen with its hood erected.

Gerald Palmer was in charge of the M.G. design office at Cowley from 1949 to 1954, during which he is best remembered for the Z-Series Magnette. This is one of his proposals for a new streamlined M.G. sports car, provisionally called the M.G. Magna, for 1954.

In 1953, the Nottingham based coachbuilders Shipsides built this one-off coupé based upon the TD Midget.

The Shipsides TD seen from the front. Note the elegant M.G. Car Club badge, the style of which is still much the same today.

Another attempt at rebodying the TD was by Ghia-Aigle of Switzerland.

The Ghia-Aigle TD was in fact quite an attractive and distinctive car with very modern, smooth lines.

When Leonard Lord rejected M.G.'s EX175 proposal for an all-new streamlined Midget, the men at Abingdon were forced to produce what was effectively a face-lifted TD. It became the TF, and this was the first prototype.

Another view of the prototype TF Midget. Note the bonnet louvres, which differed on production cars.

Launched alongside the TF at the Earls Court Motor show in 1953, the Gerald Palmer-designed Z-Type Magnette replaced the distinctly old-fashioned Y-Type. This is a full-size mock-up.

The ZA Magnette was a roomier and more comfortable sporting family saloon than the distinctly pre-war Y-Type.

A typical studio shot of a production TF Midget.

M.G.'s first all-new post-war record breaker, EX179, in original left-hand guise. Photographed prior to the trip to Utah in August 1954 where it achieved 153.69 mph.

The chassis of EX179 prior to being despatched to Midland Sheet Metal Co. for panelling. The basic chassis is the same as EX175 (HMO6).

The team of four EX182 prototypes, effectively alloy-bodied pre-production MGAs, which the factory entered in the famous Le Mans 24 Hour race of June 10/11, 1955.

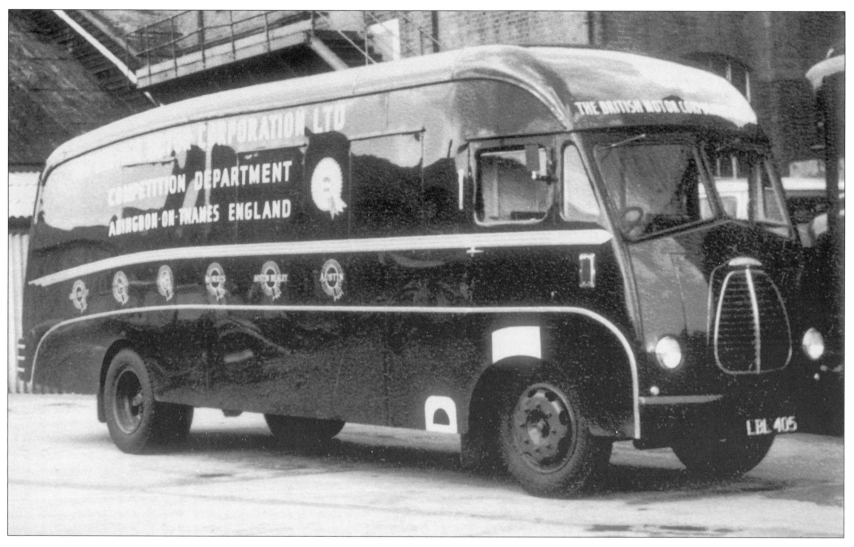

The BMC Competition Department had this specially built transporter for Le Mans. Note the registration LBL 405—in sequence with the cars themselves!

The whole party from M.G. for the 1955 Le Mans—36 people in total—was put up in a decaying French château, the Château Chêne de Cœur. Mrs. Marcus Chambers is standing to the left of the Riley Pathfinder chaperon car.

Another view of the entourage outside Château Chêne de Cœur.

From the front, the château looked suitably impressive as a backdrop to the three team cars.

Essential servicing of Ted Lund's car, LBL 303, prior to the race.

Anxious moments during scrutineering.

The three EX182 entries. Note that the wrong entry numbers have been applied. The cars were actually raced as 41, 42, and 64, whereas they appear here as 40, 41, and 64.

Ready for the off! The équipe M.G. prior to the race. Note that the cars are wearing the correct numbers at this stage.

Someone from the M.G. party saw fit to photograph the beautiful and powerful Mercedes SLR team in their neat pits prior to the race. The race would bring tragedy for Mercedes and many spectators, as Pierre Levegh crashed his 300SLR, killing himself and more than 80 spectators.

24 HEURES DU MANS - LISTE DES ENGAGÉS (d'après l'Argus)

Nº	Marque ou constructeur de la voiture	Cyl. en cm3	Conducteurs	Nº	Marque ou constructeur de la voiture	Cyl. en cm3	Conducteurs
1	Lagonda	4.487	Parnell D. Poore.	.39	Kieft	1.493	B. Baxter-J. Deeley.
. 2	Talbot	4.532	L. Rosier-X...	40	Osca	1.491	Kabianca-Scorbati.
3	Ferrari	4.412	X... X...	.41	M.G.	1.490	K. Miles-J. Lockett.
4	Ferrari	4.412	X... X...	.42	M.G.	1.490	R. Jacobs-J. Flynn.
5	Ferrari	4.412	X... X...	.43	Connaught	1.484	K. McAlpine-E. Thomson.
. 6	Jaguar	3.442	J.M. Hawthorn-Ivor Bueb.	.45	Arnott	1.097	X.-P. Taylor.
. 7	Jaguar	3.442	A.P.R. Rolt-J.D. Hamilton.	.46	Kieft	1.097	A. Rippon-R. Merrick.
. 8	Jaguar	3.442	J. Titterington-D. Beauman.	.47	Cooper	1.097	E. Wadsworth-J. Brown.
9	Jaguar	3.442	P. Walters-W. Spear.	.48	Lotus	1.097	C. Chapman-R. Flockhart.
.10	Jaguar	3.442	R. Laurent-J. Swaters.	.49	Porsche	1.090	A. Duntov-A. Veuillet.
.11	Cooper	3.442	P. Whitehead-G. Whitehead.	.50	Panhard	851	P. Chancel-R. Chancel.
.12	Ferrari	3.000	P. Heldé-J. Lucas.	.51	Panhard	851	R. Cotton-A. Beaulieux.
.14	Ferrari	3.000	M. Sparken-F. Picard.	.52	Panhard	747	P. Hémard-P. Flahault.
15	Maserati	2.991	X...-X...	.53	Panhard	747	Navarro-M. de Montrémy.
16	Maserati	2.991	X...-X...	54	Moretti	747	Linofayen-Rogenry.
17	Gordini	2.982	R. Manzon-E. Bayol.	55	Moretti	747	Ubezzi-Bellenger.
19	Mercedes	2.975	J.M. Fangio-S. Moss.	.56	V.P.	747	Y. Giraud Caban.-Y. Lesur.
20	Mercedes	2.975	X...-X...	.57	D.B.	745	X... X...
21	Mercedes	2.975	P. Levegh-J. Fitch.	.58	D.B.	745	X... X...
22	Cunningham	2.942	B.S. Cunningham-X...	.59	D.B.	745	L. Héry-G. Trouis.
23	Aston-Martin	2.922	Collins-Paul Frère.	.60	Stanguellini	740	P. Faure-P. Duval.
24	Aston-Martin	2.922	Salvadori-Walker.	.61	Nardi	735	M. Damonte-R. Crovetto.
25	Aston-Martin	2.922	Brooks-Riseley.	.62	Porsche	1.498	X... X...
.26	Austin-Healey	2.662	L. Macklin-Veston.	.63	D.B.	745	X... X...
.27	Salmson	2.328	J.P. Colas-Dewez.				
.28	Triumph	1.991	J. Dickson-N. Sanderson.		**Les 10 suppléants**		
.29	Triumph	1.991	N. Richardson-H.L. Haddeley.	.64	M.G.	1.490	E. Lund-H. Waeffler.
30	Gordini	1.987	X...-X...	.65	Porsche	1.498	J. Jeser.
31	Maserati	1.986	X...-X...	.66	Porsche	1.498	X... X...
.32	Bristol	1.979	T. Wisdom-J. Fairman.	67	Jaguar	3.442	H. Peignaux-J. Brussin.
.33	Bristol	1.979	J.C. Keen-X...	.68	Triumph	1.991	L. Brooke-J. Walton.
.34	Bristol	1.979	P. Wilson-J. Mayers.	69	Constantin ★	1.978	J. Poch-Savoye.
.35	Frazer-Nash	1.977	M. Becquart-R.S. Stoop.	.70	Ferry	746	J. Blaché-L. Pons.
.36	Frazer-Nash	1.977	R. Odlum-C. Vard.	71	Maserati	1.484	X...-X...
.37	Porsche	1.498	Polensky-V. Frankenberg.	.72	V.P.	747	Dumazer-Hechard.
.38	Porsche	1.498	W. Riggenberg-H. Gilomen.	.73	Renault	747	J.L. Rosier-J. Estager.

Courtesy of Cliff Bray, this is the complete register of entrants for the 1955 Le Mans race. M.G. No. 64 was listed as one of the "suppléants" or substitute entries, added following elimination of some entries during testing or scrutineering.

The crowded pits at Le Mans, June 1955.

The M.G. pit area at Le Mans was a hectic place to be, and a constant watch had to be kept in case of souvenir hunters.

Cliff Bray of BMC Competitions seated in one of the EX182 cars at Le Mans.

The three EX182 cars being readied in the pits at Le Mans.

During the race, the Ted Lund/Hans Waeffler car is seen pressing on through atrociously wet conditions. This car went on to finish sixth in its class.

Factory records show that LBL 303 was the car raced by Ted Lund and Hans Waeffler as No. 64 in the 1955 Le Mans race. This is almost certainly one of the Le Mans cars but, as Abingdon was not averse to swapping registration plates, it is difficult to be certain which one it was!

Early in the race, the still undamaged Lund/Waeffler EX182 (No. 64) leads the Ken Miles/Johnny Lockett car (No. 41).

Ted Lund leads a Triumph TR3 and a Porsche under the Dunlop bridge.

The Lund/Waeffler EX182 (No. 64) amidst a clutch of competitors.

Dick Jacobs' EX182 came to a tragic end at the Maison Blanche (White House), when it left the track and burst into flames in the sixth hour. Jacobs was badly hurt. Note the rather incongruous chef!

Hasty repairs to the Lund/Waeffler car during the race.

At the end of the race, a proud John Thornley (in cap) accompanies the weary crew of No. 64 past the winning line.

After the 1955 Le Mans, a team of MGAs was prepared for the Tourist Trophy race of September 17 at the Dundrod circuit in Northern Ireland. This low-headlamp prototype was fitted with the Morris Engines prototype MGA Twin Cam engine. It retired during the race.

MGAs and ZA Magnettes on the lines at Abingdon.

Standing behind the MGAs for the 33rd Mille Miglia road race of April 1956 are, left to right, Peter Scott-Russell, Tom Haig, Pat Faichney, and Nancy Mitchell. These cars finished second and third in class, Nancy Mitchell being the highest placed female driver.

Nancy Mitchell and Pat Faichney in MBL 867 prior to scrutineering for the Mille Miglia. Note the special Auster aero-screens, double-dipping rear view mirror, and additional rear view mirror to allow the co-driver to keep a look out behind.

Scrutineering prior to the 1956 Mille Miglia. Nancy Mitchell looks on anxiously. The Mille Miglia was a gruelling 992 mile long road race, with Rome as the half-way point and with the finish, like the start, at Brescia.

The weather during the 1956 Mille Miglia was very bad. The rain poured down continuously and water streamed into the cockpits of the open MGAs. This is Nancy Mitchell driving MBL 867, with Pat Faichney as navigator.

Nancy Mitchell drives through the heavy rain. The race number "227" signifies the start time of 2:27 a.m. at Brescia, Northern Italy. Mitchell and Faichney were the highest placed female team in the race. They covered 992 miles in 15 hours, 7 minutes and 28 seconds!

Nancy Mitchell and Pat Faichney in MBL 867 during the six day long Rallye des Alpes in July 1956. Nancy went on to achieve third in her class, 15th place overall and won the ladies prize.

The Alpine scenery was a spectacular back-drop to the Rallye des Alpes.

Nancy Mitchell and Pat Faichney's MGA pictured during the Rallye des Alpes.

The Rallye des Alpes took in more than just spectacular mountain passes, as this photo shows.

A rest stop shared by three of the MGAs, and, amongst others, a Porsche and two British Ford Zephyr Mk. IIs.

Three of the five-car MGA team entered by the factory for the July 1956 Rallye des Alpes, including MBL 867 (nearest camera, with Nancy Mitchell behind).

Nancy Mitchell (driving) and Pat Faichney (co-driver) at the start of the 1956 XVIII Rallye des Alpes.

Nancy Mitchell receives her "Coupe des Dames" at the conclusion of the race. Nancy also won — in common with all finishers — a coveted "Coupe des Alpes", making her only the third woman to have won such an award in the 17 years that the race had been run.

Some thirty years after its 1956 escapades, British M.G. enthusiasts Bob West and Mike Horner spent five years restoring MBL 867—"Mabel"—to her former Mille Miglia glory.

EX179 in right-hand drive guise with, left to right, Tom Haig, Bunny Hillier, Jimmy Cox, Cliff Bray, Henry Stone, Alec Hounslow, and engineering chief Syd Enever.

In the wake of the 1955 Le Mans tragedy, BMC had toned down M.G.'s racing activities in Europe. This was not so in the USA, however. Americans Fred Allen and John Van Driel took turns in this MGA, one of a team of three, at Sebring in March 1956. The MGAs went on to win the team prize.

In the pits at Sebring. The car in the foreground was driven by Americans Gus Ehrman and David Ash to 5th in class and 20th overall.

New in 1956 was the coupé version of the MGA. This is actually a 1600 of 1959—the side lamps give the secret away—but otherwise the 1500 was externally almost identical.

This model shows the Frua proposal for a rebodied MGA, complete with removable coupé hardtop. The model survives in the Heritage collection.

The lines of the Frua MGA were very attractive, but M.G. were formulating their own ideas for a monocoque MGB.

From the rear, the Frua MGA bears a resemblance to the Aston Martin DB4. The full-size prototype also came with a hard-top, which survived the actual prototype for some time before being lost.

The finished Frua-bodied MGA resembled a contemporary Maserati. It was eventually cut up with acetylene torches, in order to avoid payment of import taxes.

These three 1/4 scale models show the thought processes which led to the MGB. They are, left to right, the Frua bodied MGA (listed under code EX205), an early separate chassis MGB prototype (also EX205), and one of the first monocoque MGB ideas (EX214).

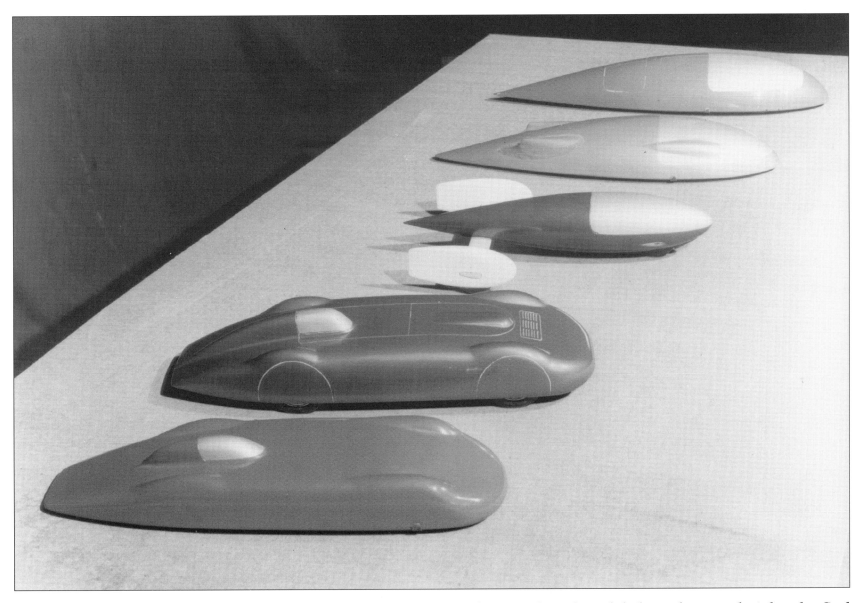

Harry Herring was M.G.'s model maker at Abingdon, and he often produced models based upon sketches by Syd Enever. This is a selection of "Record Breakers".

EX181 was the all-new M.G. Record Breaker for 1957. Designed by Syd Enever, the car was drawn up by chassis engineer Terry Mitchell. Seated in the cock-pit is Stirling Moss; crouched down at the extreme right is John Thornley, whilst Syd Enever is bending over to the left of Thornley.

Behind Stirling Moss in the cockpit of EX181 are
John Thornley, at left, and Syd Enever.

The MGA Twin Cam featured an engine based upon the B-Series used in the MGA but extensively re-worked.

The twin cam engine was a tight fit in the MGA engine bay.

The Pininfarina-styled Magnette Mk. III was launched on November 18, 1958. Built at Cowley, it had no real M.G. pedigree and was not a popular car. This is a pre-production car. The ADO9G registration plate was false, denoting project code ADO9, with the "G" signifying M.G.

In 1959, the MGA became the MGA 1600, with an enlarged B-Series engine.

At Le Mans, Ted Lund drove this twin cam engined MGA. It was based upon one of the 1955 Le Mans cars, believed to be Car. No. 64, as raced in 1955 by Lund himself. Ted Lund is seen leaning against the driver's side of the car before the start of the race.

The engine bay of Ted Lund's MGA Twin Cam, SRX 210. Note the hand-written dedication to M.G.'s engine builder Jimmy Cox.

What Ted Lund had hoped to race at Le Mans was EX186, seen here bearing so-called "trade plates" used for road-testing this unlicensed vehicle on public roads.

The following series of photographs were taken by Denis Williams, proud draughtsman who created its sleek lines.

The original plan was to build about ten of these special De Dion rear axle racing cars. In the end, only this one was built.

Inspiration for the MGA-based EX186 clearly came from both the D-Type Jaguar and the Mercedes SLR.

The cockpit of EX186 was practical and purposeful.

Close-up view of EX186's dashboard, showing the single large instrument, a tachometer, and various smaller temperature and pressure gauges.

Dickie Wright took this photograph of EX186, which shows off the car's very long tapered tail.

EX205, M.G.'s thoughts for an MGB, was the work of Chief Body Engineer Jim O'Neill.

The O'Neill design resembled the Aston Martin DB4.

In October 1959, American ace driver Phil Hill took the M.G. record breaker, EX181, to 254.91 mph at Utah, smashing six two-litre speed records in the process.

Phil Hill (in white overalls) stands to the right of Captain George Eyston, the celebrated record breaker, behind EX181.

EX181 at speed on the salt flats. Note the black oil line, used to guide driver Phil Hill on the otherwise almost featureless plain.

Carroll Shelby seated in an abortive prototype for the EX219 record breaker, to have been based upon the Austin-Healey Sprite. The aerodynamics were hopeless and the idea was abandoned.

Historians often misunderstand this photograph. It celebrates the 50,000th sports car produced at Abingdon in 1959 —not the 50,000th sports car ever produced there! The car is an export MGA 1600.

104

SRX 210 returned to Le Mans in June 1960, with new aerodynamic coupé bodywork designed by Don Hayter. It is seen here during scrutineering.

SRX 210 en route to Le Mans.

Transport for the Ted Lund équipe was slightly less grand than that boasted by the larger factory teams!

The proud team with SRX 210 prior to the race.

The Ted Lund MGA at the M.G. pits.

BMC at Longbridge played with the idea of an M.G. based upon the Mini on a number of occasions. This is a full-size mock-up dating from 1960.

The special coupé bodied MGA Twin Cam raced in the last of its three trips to Le Mans in this form in 1961. It is seen here some years after the race, but still more or less in 1961 trim.

The aerodynamic nose of SRX 210, Ted Lund's Le Mans MGA, as raced at the 1961 race.

Note the large Le Mans fuel filler recessed into the swept back tail of the car.

SRX 210 photographed at the M.G. factory in 1961. Note the then new Austin-Healey Sprite Mk. II's in the background, along with Morris Minor vans, then also being assembled at Abingdon.

Ted Lund, Le Mans, June 1961.

Ted Lund's MGA is admired by spectators prior to its final 1961 Le Mans foray.

SRX 210 en route to Le Mans.

The major M.G. event of 1962 was the launch at the Earls Court Motor Show of the MGB roadster and M.G. 1100 saloon, sold in the USA as the Sports Sedan.

Renault accused BMC of plagiarising their Floride for the styling of the MGB. Judge for yourself....

Photographed in October 1961, this is one of the pre-production prototype MGB roadsters, now virtually in production form. Note the lack of front bumper over-riders, initially listed as an optional extra on home-market cars but soon fitted as standard.

256 GBL was an early factory MGB demonstrator, which was used for some time by Dickie Wright of M.G., who took this contemporary photograph in the Cotswolds.

This is a pre-production prototype of the UK-market M.G. 1100, photographed in November 1961. Briefly considered as a name for this car was the MGC 1100.

In 1963, Syd Enever and Jim Stimson designed this longer, more aerodynamic nose for the MGB when used in long distance races. It is seen here on BMO 541B, being crewed by Andrew Hedges and John Sprinzel on the 1964 Tour de France Automobile.

Predating the official MGB GT of 1965 was this offering by the Belgian coachbuilder Jacques Coune. This actual car was built for a BMC executive and appraised by the company.

This is actually the 1965 Le Mans race, but the 1964 MGB for Le Mans was very similar.

This is the Longbridge built version of the Mini-based M.G. sports car concept ADO34, with styling by Pininfarina.

The Pininfarina detailed MGB GT prototype, photographed in June 1964.

The Iconografix Photo Archive Series includes:

AMERICAN CULTURE

AMERICAN SERVICE STATIONS 1935-1943	ISBN 1-882256-27-1
COCA-COLA: A HISTORY IN PHOTOGRAPHS 1930-1969	ISBN 1-882256-46-8
COCA-COLA: ITS VEHICLES IN PHOTOGRAPHS 1930-1969	ISBN 1-882256-47-6
PHILLIPS 66 1945-1954	ISBN 1-882256-42-5

AUTOMOTIVE

IMPERIAL 1955-1963	ISBN 1-882256-22-0
IMPERIAL 1964-1968	ISBN 1-882256-23-9
LE MANS 1950: THE BRIGGS CUNNINGHAM CAMPAIGN	ISBN 1-882256-21-2
PACKARD MOTOR CARS 1935-1942	ISBN 1-882256-44-1
PACKARD MOTOR CARS 1946-1958	ISBN 1-882256-45-X
SEBRING 12-HOUR RACE 1970	ISBN 1-882256-20-4
STUDEBAKER 1933-1942	ISBN 1-882256-24-7
STUDEBAKER 1946-1958	ISBN 1-882256-25-5
LINCOLN MOTOR CARS 1920-1942	ISBN 1-882256-57-3
LINCOLN MOTOR CARS 1946-1960	ISBN 1-882256-58-1
MG 1945-1964	ISBN 1-882256-52-2
MG 1965-1980	ISBN 1-882256-53-0

TRACTORS AND CONSTRUCTION EQUIPMENT

CASE TRACTORS 1912-1959	ISBN 1-882256-32-8
CATERPILLAR MILITARY TRACTORS VOLUME 1	ISBN 1-882256-16-6
CATERPILLAR MILITARY TRACTORS VOLUME 2	ISBN 1-882256-17-4
CATERPILLAR SIXTY	ISBN 1-882256-05-0
CATERPILLAR THIRTY	ISBN 1-882256-04-2
CLETRAC AND OLIVER CRAWLERS	ISBN 1-882256-43-3
FARMALL F-SERIES	ISBN 1-882256-02-6
FARMALL MODEL H	ISBN 1-882256-03-4
FARMALL MODEL M	ISBN 1-882256-15-8
FARMALL REGULAR	ISBN 1-882256-14-X

FARMALL SUPER SERIES	ISBN 1-882256-49-2
FORDSON 1917-1928	ISBN 1-882256-33-6
HART-PARR	ISBN 1-882256-08-5
HOLT TRACTORS	ISBN 1-882256-10-7
INTERNATIONAL TRACTRACTOR	ISBN 1-882256-48-4
JOHN DEERE MODEL A	ISBN 1-882256-12-3
JOHN DEERE MODEL B	ISBN 1-882256-01-8
JOHN DEERE MODEL D	ISBN 1-882256-00-X
JOHN DEERE 30 SERIES	ISBN 1-882256-13-1
MINNEAPOLIS-MOLINE U-SERIES	ISBN 1-882256-07-7
OLIVER TRACTORS	ISBN 1-882256-09-3
RUSSELL GRADERS	ISBN 1-882256-11-5
TWIN CITY TRACTOR	ISBN 1-882256-06-9

RAILWAYS

GREAT NORTHERN RAILWAY 1945-1970	ISBN 1-882256-56-5
MILWAUKEE ROAD 1850-1960	ISBN 1-882256-61-1

TRUCKS

BEVERAGE TRUCKS 1910-1975	ISBN 1-882256-60-3
BROCKWAY TRUCKS 1948-1961	ISBN 1-882256-55-7
DODGE TRUCKS 1929-1947	ISBN 1-882256-36-0
DODGE TRUCKS 1948-1960	ISBN 1-882256-37-9
LOGGING TRUCKS 1915-1970	ISBN 1-882256-59-X
MACK MODEL AB	ISBN 1-882256-18-2
MACK AP SUPER DUTY TRKS 1926-1938	ISBN 1-882256-54-9
MACK MODEL B 1953-1966 VOLUME 1	ISBN 1-882256-19-0
MACK MODEL B 1953-1966 VOLUME 2	ISBN 1-882256-34-4
MACK EB-EC-ED-EE-EF-EG-DE 1936-1951	ISBN 1-882256-29-8
MACK EH-EJ-EM-EQ-ER-ES 1936-1950	ISBN 1-882256-39-5
MACK FC-FCSW-NW 1936-1947	ISBN 1-882256-28-X
MACK FG-FH-FJ-FK-FN-FP-FT-FW 1937-1950	ISBN 1-882256-35-2
MACK LF-LH-LJ-LM-LT 1940-1956	ISBN 1-882256-38-7
STUDEBAKER TRUCKS 1927-1940	ISBN 1-882256-40-9
STUDEBAKER TRUCKS 1941-1964	ISBN 1-882256-41-7

The Iconografix Photo Archive Series is available from direct mail specialty book dealers and bookstores worldwide, or can be ordered from the publisher. For additional information or to add your name to our mailing list contact:

Iconografix
PO Box 609/Bk
Osceola, Wisconsin 54020 USA

Telephone: (715) 294-2792
(800) 289-3504 (USA)
Fax: (715) 294-3414

Book trade distribution by Voyageur Press, Inc., PO Box 338, Stillwater, Minnesota 55082 USA (800) 888-9653
European distribution by Midland Publishing Limited, 24 The Hollow, Earl Shilton, Leicester LE9 7N1 England

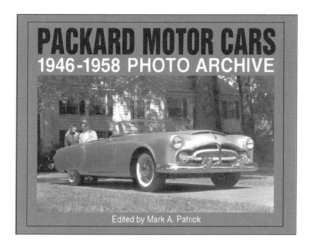

PACKARD MOTOR CARS
1946-1958 PHOTO ARCHIVE

Edited by Mark A. Patrick

MORE
GREAT BOOKS FROM
ICONOGRAFIX

PACKARD MOTOR CARS 1946-1958
Photo Archive ISBN 1-882256-45-X

MG 1965-1980 *Photo Archive*
ISBN 1-882256-53-0

SEBRING 12-HOUR RACE 1970 *Photo
Archive* ISBN 1-882256-20-4

**LE MANS 1950: PHOTO ARCHIVE
THE BRIGGS CUNNINGHAM CAMPAIGN**
ISBN 1-882256-21-2

MACK MODEL B 1953-66 VOLUME 1
Photo Archive ISBN 1-882256-19-0

**COCA-COLA: A HISTORY IN PHOTO-
GRAPHS 1930-1969**
ISBN 1-882256-46-8

**AMERICAN SERVICE STATIONS
1935-1943** *Photo Archive*
ISBN 1-882256-27-1

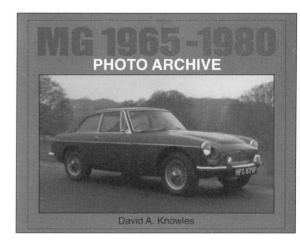

MG 1965-1980
PHOTO ARCHIVE

David A. Knowles

SEBRING 12-HOUR RACE 1970
PHOTO ARCHIVE

Edited by Robert C. Auten

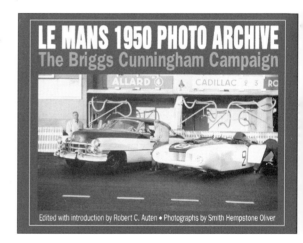

LE MANS 1950 PHOTO ARCHIVE
The Briggs Cunningham Campaign

Edited with introduction by Robert C. Auten • Photographs by Smith Hempstone Oliver

MACK MODEL B 1953-1966
VOLUME 1 PHOTO ARCHIVE

Edited by Thomas E. Warth

Coca-Cola
A HISTORY IN PHOTOGRAPHS 1930-1969

Howard Applegate

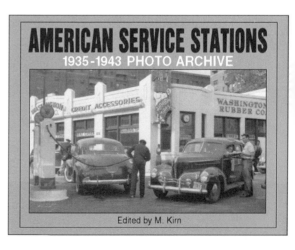

AMERICAN SERVICE STATIONS
1935-1943 PHOTO ARCHIVE

Edited by M. Kirn